Sweet City Cares

Poetry

Andrea Elizabeth De Graaf

The toils, abstracts & memories of our hearts

SWEET CITY CARES

 Printed in the United States of America. For information write to PO Box 202 Lowell Michigan 49331.

info@andreadegraaf.com

Cover designed by Andrea Elizabeth De Graaf

ISBN: 978-1-7358974-2-4

Dedication

As I breathe, I write.

To all the people in my life whose love and support made this life enjoyable. Thank you kindly.

TABLE OF CONTENTS

Preface

Thank God who is greatest above all for his blessings.

I wrote this book of poetry *Sweet City Cares* just for you, thought by thought, word by word and page by page. I hope that every one who reads this work will enjoy it.

Thank you and God bless you.

Andrea Elizabeth De Graaf

Sleep

When you lie at night
I hope you find the best side of sleep.

I Use to Know a Boy

I use to know a boy
we walked to school hand in hand when we were ten,
then I was twenty, he brought me to the movies,
I ate popcorn and laughed while he laid on my shoulder and smiled.
When I reached thirty, he gave me a pendant
we graduated from college and looked forward to forty.
At forty, we were walking down the street
when a lady said hello to him with a smile,
he released my hand and walked with her past our destination.
Here comes fifty, the turbulent plane seemed to be going down,
my child in my hands and the air hostess in his.
Sixty, O my, I looked like forty, what a time I had,
he looked like himself.
Seventy, we are happy, our children are older now,
we walked hand in hand down the street,
young ladies passed by, he never let go.
And so, eighty, ninety, we are still holding on to each other with no desire to let go.

A Girl I Knew

There was a girl I knew, she was black, white and blue.
She had opened eyes and a dynamite smile.
I met a guy last night; one she would have liked--
not so much for a ride, but for a long, long drive.
I got up this morning early to meet that girl again,
when I started to wonder if she was still my friend.

Each day I waited to meet her, with gear and saddles on,
but the guy I thought she would have liked
had passed sometime along.
In three months or four, I walked in front of my door,
I saw the girl standing there, hard to the core.
Her hair short and dreaded, her arms as shiny as gold,
her legs, long and flary and her gut as flat as the floor.
I asked her many questions about her toils and actions,
she echoed and smiled, then we ran upstairs to my husband.

My Backyard

There was a man who lived in my backyard,
I didn't know him very well,
but I sometimes saw him on Tuesdays.
He would run about in wide circles
and up and down my backyard,
then he would stop for a while
and observe all that was around him.
I thought to take his picture
but that seemed like an invasion.
He was busier with nature,
than with thoughts about me.
I retreated to my kitchen
and my thoughts back to me.
What will I make for breakfast?
and who will edit this book for me.

Grace

God gives me grace to fill up my spaces
God gives me grace to deal with the races.

Would You Tell Me

I watched you walk away with not much fuss.
I guessed that you were tired.
Tired of you, tired of me, tired of the world around you,
but I wondered why you never said in any way
that life made you dismayed on any day.
What was the delay?
I seem to want to know if my time with you was too much
or my walk with you too little.
Would you tell me?
For time doesn't speak much to wonderers
in the laundromat, when everyone's eyes are on the hand of time.

Tree Song

So beautiful it is outside,
glittering snow, golden trees,
sure footprints in the snow,
yet my heart aches with sadness
like the lonely tree whose limb
has been broken by the weight
of the white snow.

I watched the tree dance,
as the snow began.
Happily, it held its limbs, high snow and low snow,
all stacked upon each other.
The limb held it mightily, then gave way.
On the ground the limb lay, the snow notices not.
How lonely is the tree, that green tree?
How lonely are we.

Can Someone Find Me

Can someone find me?
The stones in my eyes shine
and my heart is leaking upon my face.
My rescue boat left without picking me up.
I'm holding on to a tree's bark
but I can feel it fading.
My heart is sinking like July's sky.
Can someone find me?
My mother, my father, my uncle,
the man whom I have never seen.
Only in my dreams he dares to tread.

If You Find Me

If you find me, don't tell anyone.
Let me rest a little,
let the world wait for me a while.
If you find me, don't write my name
or wonder why or how,
for God and men are not sound.
If you find me, lay my head on a rock--
not on your divided shoulders,
and light me a fire.
If you find me, lay beside me.
Open not the box as I sleep;
it'll be too early for our decay.
If you find me, tell me not your troubles.
Go dip into the river
then say your prayers.
If you find me, be still
know that we have been reborn.
Let's weep no more like sinners do,
for God and men are unalike.

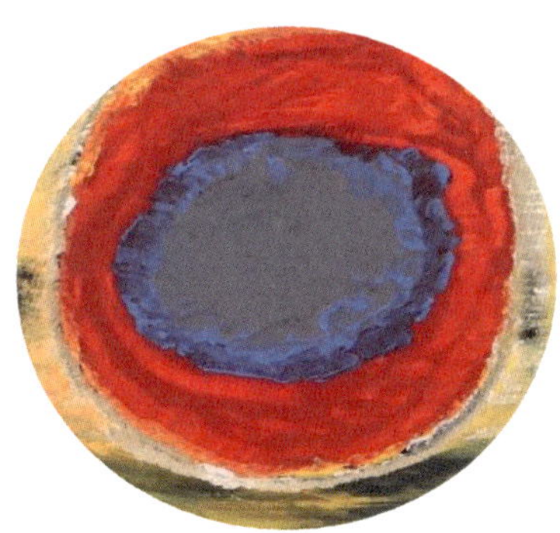

Decline

We started as Generals.
Together we protected each other on the battlefield.
All problems were timely.
We conspired against the enemy
and upheld the principles of our nation,
our stars shining brightly for all to see.

As the years passed by,
I saw the lieutenant performing as one should,
consuming the thoughts of the general:
head up, chin forward,
duties completed, honorably discharged.

Today we protect the nation
not by principles but by duty.
Like the Lieutenant, I patrol the grounds, a team of one.
I get my untimely information as needed,
without threats of insubordination and dishonorable
discharge.
We started as Generals.

Age

How old are you?
I have an age or two.
The funny thing is that it is true.
Look at me today,
then look at me tomorrow,
and the same thing will happen to you.

Scrappy Babies

Why peep at mine with empty arms?
Giggles and waits for a touch
wiggling, prancing, sword to your face
with all those souls attached to you.
I made no promises, I told no stories.
Must I feel guilty for you? For them?
What you feel—must I take responsibility,
then apologize in a trendy way?
Who? Who? Who is to blame?
Is it God, your mother, your father?
Should I have mercy and give you a cloth?
I cannot dry the blood that drips from those souls.
I must turn my back at this age,
though it's not my tradition; my spirit will be at peace.
Your plagues will not serve me.
I will not bear witness to your naked flesh.
You must go now—take your empty arms and fill them with Myrrh,
recompense your choices, for none can pay for breath never taken.

Insurance Lost

Too many baskets in my head,
my in-basket is over flowing and my net has holes.
I pay my insurance for coverage
but I am denied when I fall.
Come, make my needs skilled,
place me into that category where nets are mended.
Take away my chronic illness
and do not make my needs custodial.
What mighty chair the powerful sit in.
Twirling, contemplating our sick fate.
Oh, followers with the red pens
review and deny them to the end.
Dear Newborn:
You are recommended to get one skilled nursing visit
and we all must consent.
If diagnosis grim for you must be,
the Medical Director, so far, you "auth" to see.
But where do I find him?
The lady in the Philippines said,
"Only peer to peer review the Medical director will do."

Covid Covid COVID-19

Covid Covid COVID-19
        You are a sneaky one
You plugged my nose
        With my own hands
And almost let me fry my brain pan.

White Hole

There is a white hole that's filled with climbers,
each trying to reach the top to show its head.
There is black at the top,
white behind.
Alphabet's rights on the line.
Now adoption has the rope,
hunger is trying,
crime is climbing,
politicians are morphing,
common sense is falling,
morals lay dying.
In the bottom of the hole
Health Care sits,
waiting for them all to fall,
that it may kill them all.

Detained Sight

Congratulations. I saw it in his eyes.
How long has it been?
"Has it been always, yesterday or just today?"
I heard his questions. What hostility.
Where did it come from?
To whom did he surrender?
I removed my eyes in silence, but he knew I heard him.
I felt his stare burning into my hurt.
I moved away from his venom.
He was a first-time witness, a victim of not being around.
He left as a wonderer—what he saw,
I do not wish to clarify for him
the beholding of his sight.
He felt it and his own feelings he must surely know.

The Woman on the Left

The woman to the left seemed to fancy Jeff
but my boyfriend, to the right,
tried to wander into her sight.
He brushed his hair and moved his chair,
ordered her champagne and gave me beer.
He recommended lobster plus a seafood platter
as he sat there nibbling at the batter.
I could not move my spine was numb,
my tongue felt heavy like a lump of chewing gum,
my friend sat there joking while I was choking,
then they got up, left, and stuck me with the check.
I was a reck.

When I got home, I was a mess.
My boyfriend looked at me and said, "Why did you leave?"
I went and took a shower to regain my power
for tomorrow sometime, will be my hour.

My boyfriend on the right has a handsome half brother
whom the woman on the left wished to devour,
I called him late and told him straight
so, he decided to give me a holler.
Then I called Marlene who loved to scheme and has a trillion dollars,
when morning came, my plan was done and ready for a run.

The pilot went for the woman on the left
and told her my boyfriend's story.
The huge house and stores with Gucci blouses
and oil rigs to make her come faster.
Then she went home with plenty of moans
elated in her unknown disaster.

She quit her job, got into a cab to where I lay my slipper.
She knocked on my door and with one big roar,
she smacked me on my shoulder.
My boyfriend got up and calmed her down
then asked her what's the matter.

The woman on the left said,
"Honey let her leave; I can treat you better."
She took the bait and will meet her fate,
because my boyfriend doesn't have a dollar.
My boyfriend turned around and threw me out
and that was the end of the matter.

Silas

I dream of Silas and I dream of you.
I told my friends and they said not to tell you.
I told my priest and he said,"
"What are you going to do?"
I told my sister and she said,
"You know what to do."
I was about to tell my neighbor
but he said, "How do you do?"
Picking up sticks and stones and bricks
I throw them hard and far,
hoping to relieve the anxiety of something I did not do.
My husband came and started throwing with me,
one stone, one stick and one brick.
I said, "Honey, I dream of Silas and I dream of you."
My husband said, "Honey, I dream of Paul too."

Preformed Heart

These are the nothings that lead to somethings.
You are silly, acting stupid and nagging,
when the question is, "Where did you put the juice?"
It is simple. And what somethings do those words lead to?
I don't know, but I will be armed when I find out.

I open my eyes to the nothing,
and make preparations for the something
for time exempts the master
then delivers the unprepared to the slaughter.
I do not fuss anymore,
my heart renders the hurt in icy form,
enough for me to handle.
My tears do not flow so freely,
not even behind closed doors.
I bind my words--not to suffocate,
but enough to maintain my peace.

Why act like a stranger?
Why take the dream of my many conversations?
Who do you lay upon my bed? I moved my fingers,
unable to count the seemingly uncountable occurrences of apologies.
I will go to our bridge now--where we use to meet,
just as before without a plan. I have a preformed heart.

The Watchman

I lay not for you, I lay not for me,
but for defiance, for my priest.
For every day that I work and want to get up and run but had to stay.
I lay for the sacrifices that I made.
I do not flinch, for life is such and moments speak and moments are unforgiving.
I do not envy the look you give, so sure that I don't see.
The accidental touch upon her arm,
the tormented anger which grows like a fruit tree whenever she displeases,
The joy that consumes your face when she behaves.
But I lay for her as well.
How brief, short and painful our conversations are,
though polite and accommodating
since my willing partner exchange
you have already had before you got home.
I hurried my words, tick-tock, I better make it fast,
"How was your day?" That's fast enough,
tick-tock, no more—it is time to listen.
Merry Christmas! Happy New Year!
I know them well; they were mine, as I slept.
Now I awaken to see that the world had them all along.
Haha, I laugh for the watchman,
for all the noes I give each day.
In the calmest of moments, I dare not surrender--
as I lay for her future—when he is awake.

The Invited

I asked a fish to go home with me and he said,
"Only if you give me water and promise not to scale me."
I invited a goat home, and he said,
"Only if you give me no water and promise not to curry me."
I asked a squirrel home and he said,
"No nut jokes and don't ask me to spread my bed."
A snake was nearby but I ignored him instead.
The snake said,
"I can slither on by and you won't even know that I am not dead."
I looked at the snake wanting to kick it in the head,
but I saw a man coming and I knew I wanted to wed.
I invited the man home and he said,
"Only if you give me water, feed me meat, give me nut-things and put me to sleep."
I got up the next morning only to find my fish without a fin in a bin,
my goat in a rope,
my squirrel on the bed without a head,
and the man on the floor behind the door.
I took up the phone to call the police
when out came the snake holding a rake. He said,
"You did not invite me home, but make no mistake, make that phone call and it will be your fate."
I looked at the snake and truly knew why the Good Lord trampled it under his feet,
but I also knew that I could not call the police.

The Two Prostitutes in My Life

I have had prostitutes before, but they never needed that much.
They just hung out on the sidelines with not much to say--
but now, I have to pay either way.
The first prostitute in my life I met when I was in college.
I had paid about $2000 from my pocket for the introduction,
and the government paid the other $2000 for services
completed for the rest of the year.
Until I graduated, the cost of this prostitute just went up and up and up.
I had to pay fees; I paid for expensive books, I signed promissory notes,
sat through hours and hours of boring lectures.
I did mathematics: and took on a second job
just to support my prostitute.
I worked hard and harder each semester,
hoping to keep my prostitute happy.
Then one day I made a mistake and he said,
"I am going to go down and you will have to work twice as hard to bring me up."
In the future, all will question your mistakes and you will have to prove that you are not fake.
That prostitute was my GPA.

The second prostitute in my life I had to deal with after I got married.

I never had one before at my house door, but my husband thought it would be wise to get one inside.
I contracted with the three major brothels at first,
but they would leave nothing in my purse,
trying to haul me into a Hearst.
So, I got rid of two, knowing that I would need one in a few.
I later called the 1-888 number to get rid of him as well,
only to have him put me through hell.
I thought I was in the clear, but my prostitute was always in the rear,
I pretended not to care, but my husband said, "Put on your gear."
I tried to change my job, but I was robbed,
I tried to buy a car but I was barred,
I armed myself with 40% to buy a home
but my prostitute hunted me down, dredged deep in my ground,
excavated my past and hollowed me out for the bank to see, but not for free.
I could not run, for my credit report had the gun; another prostitute I couldn't outrun.
I hope that someday, they will get rid of the GPA and the Supreme court will abolish credit reports.
The two prostitutes in my life.

GPA

I was walking down the street one day
when I happened to see my GPA.
He asked me out for a drink and I said no without a blink.
He stretched and stretched like nobody knows,
so much so, that he was almost comatose.
I left him in school, hoping never to see him again.
I moved away that very same day
singing praises, "Oh how I didn't have to pay."
I sat in my new home on the first day of May
enjoy the beauty of Pelham Bay.
I strutted and danced to the Reggae beat,
not paying attention to the heat.
The doorbell rang and with a bang
my GPA knocked me down with his hand.
I got up straight, no time to wait
but my GPA was quick to retaliate.
He yelled, "Rape, please come to my gate."
then he got a pencil and stabbed me in the toe.
He grabbed a rope and thinking there was no hope,
I used my knife and zapped him in the eye.
I then got the rope and hung him on the door,
then buried him under the bathroom floor.
My GPA ended when I settled the score.

Give Him Back

Where is he? The guy who was here talking to my family.
Why did you let him go?
He was patient and attentive,
hanging onto every word that they said,
he was wild and charming, full of laughter and delight.
Why did you send him away?
Where did you put him?
I know him. He likes me. I desire him. I need him. Go get him.
I know you love me, you told me but I want him.
Did you lend him out because of grief?
Who are you mourning? Did you make him invisible from me—but why?
Will you bring him back if I take you to your favorite places:
Greece, Palestine, Iran and Mali?
I won't even mention Israel.
Do you know I am in love with him?
I remove the bone from my side for him—
though temporary—I give it my all.
I will go to sleep now and when I wake up,
I will see him smiling down at me.

Gate Keeper

I reach the gate and the gate keeper is awake,
but he does not seem to see the route that I am on.
I must go through his territory, an open border by day if you pay.
I am standing with my hand stretched out, ready to pay but there is a delay.
The gate keeper waves a kind hand in my direction,
then he points a mean finger for me to go in the other.

Into Tomorrow

Into tomorrow where no man delays,
children gather around and start to pray.
Mothers don't know and fathers won't go,
into tomorrow where time tick-tock, tick-tock.

I see the pink lady and watch the blue man
calling all people telling them, "I am the one,"
come vote for me and you will see,
all will be well; you will be free.

What hammering words the blue man nails
amidst the pink lady's cries,
unmoved we edge the sea and watch the tides,
as the waves come crashing by.

Some say the pink lady went first,
others, the blue man,
tick-tock the wave has come
the house is opened—the pledge must be recited.

The Supremes looked dazed as the speaker's hand rises.
He lifts no sword, mobilizes no army; his tongue is safe.
Now he must lead all—into tomorrow, where the children pray.

AE DE GRAAF 12-20

Ooh Little Child

Ooh little child
I thought I saw your feet tapping at my song
I looked around but you were gone
as I sat and hide from the sun.
I felt the warmth of your hand on mine,
someone told me it was my imagination.
But ooh little child, I think I miss you so
I want to cover you at my age
but you are long gone and I never saw your face.
Your voice I never heard
but your silence spoke too often.
Remember me without distress,
tears, I have none left.
I will send you a dove with my pillow.
Kneel on it for my intercession--
breathe for me somewhere in heaven.
Ooh little child.

Into Tomorrow II

Oh, how we master the fruitlessness of our labor,
holding tight, unable to let go.
We squeeze it down to our graves.
Heavenly Father, hear me whisper,
I have traveled the tunnels into tomorrow.
Should I tell and lose my sleep
to avaricious men who yearn to acquire?
War and peace—not to mention power,
while scheming to get into Valhalla.
Though life is sweet and bitter be,
missionaries have hope for you and me,
fighting, writing, caring for the dying.
I have traveled the tunnels into tomorrow,
and returned the time that I borrowed.

The Fall

“Don’t fall off that high horse of yours.”
Then I went and fell right into the seat
of that air hostess with my son in my arms.

The Catch

How beautiful she was,
laying there in long brown swirl,
almost gutted and unknown.
Her head to the side, shoulders bare,
just like me, I suppose.
I was not there, I did not see
the beginning of the Malaise.
But as I approached, there he stood,
casting his net for another catch.
"Oh no!" I said, "Not today, she belongs to me."
"But why?" he said,
"The catch was clean—the law is coming you'll see,"
I looked at him and explained,
"You see, she must be free. We do not need a decree."

Color You

I do not fancy your new smile.
There are colors in between.
Purple and blue, maybe red.
What can I do for you?

I take another look it's green and white,
the thing on your nose, is it for fright?
Your face and hands are pink and black,
patchy and mismatched.
Did you change those too?

What stormy dreams you must have,
to look upon the face of God,
not knowing what color, you wish to have.

To My Lady with the Freckles

They say that you are not the star anymore
That your lights have gone dim
That your flames have burnt out and your crown has drowned.

Be watchful; six feet is far enough—under.

Showman Brownson

Showman Brownson never called my name
because he didn't want to cause any trouble
Showman Brownson only pointed me out
because he had to go on the double.
Mother Mary, I called, "Where did you stash your son?"
For mine is somewhere out there on the run
and Showman Brownson is not done.

I Am Black

I rummaged through the hill of my mind
trying to find a safe place.
The hunters are coming
and my companion is on the other side.

Who can save me? I turned my feet
to the side, hoping to disguise,
but my trackers aren't far behind
and my companion is on the other side.

Will my savior be the wolf?
The sheep are just standing by,
cold, hard, lending me no cover.
Who? Who will they devour?

The hill was once warm,
filled with safe passages;
now I am yearning for one and my mother is gone.
I whisper to my heart, but he couldn't hear me.

I remember church on Sundays—have faith.
I feel the steel at my back
and as it reflects in the sun,
I do not wait for the cock to crow.

The wolves are here. I see them.
I run to them and they run to me.
The cock goes off, I move to the side,
my hunters are home. A wolf is down.
I reach the other side,

my companion is not; I turn around,
my companion is down; the pack is on the attack,
Lord—I am black.

Crayons

My crayons are black,
every time I draw a picture,
I put them in a stack.
I like to draw on different papers.
I am always on top.
But each time I go to the bathroom,
my teacher changes my stock,
so, I go up to her and say,
"Ms., please give them back."
My crayons are black.

The West Wing

There is war in the West Wing,
which is not a strange thing.
So, the President walked over and gave a spin.
Judy in the closet, O'Connor against the door,
Sandra on the bathroom floor, Bouthman got the finger,
Mitch got a fist, but Mary got away before the President
found the rope,
many people thought that; that was dope.
Cyrus was bleeding and Ashley pleading,
but Maggie was okay because she was cheating.

The First Lady walked in with wide eyed surprise
but the President handed her a contract so she closed her eyes.
Advisor Clay quit while stating, "I don't know how to clean
this up."
But scheming Bran who was right at hand, said,
"Let's give it over to Mr. Dan."
Mr. Dan felt the pressure to do the right thing,
yet he was afraid that the President would give him a fling.
So, Mr. Dan confirmed that a mysterious world wind,
had hit the West Wing.

Reporters cluttered for a word or two and asked the
President,
"What are you going to do?"
"Win I guess," he told them straight, "Just ask my running
mate."
One reporter shouted,
"I meant, what are you going to do about what happened in
the West Wing?"
The President answered, "Depending on the signs, I will go
south, we will see, when I know you will know."

The reporters were confused, the people were weary, but the President was happy.
What happened in the West Wing, was just another thing.

Senators on the Branch

We watched the senators sitting on a branch,
flapping their wings without a song to sing.
One tried to fly, but got hit in the eye
Oh, what a flake! That must have been his fate.
One senator went out on the limb then started to sing,
the speaker came and clipped his wings.
Oh people! what a dreadful thing.
We must wonder, what's the next blunder?
Do we care or even fear?
We discard our hearts and usurp our spirits,
trying not to be the one we must see.
We watched the senators on the branch,
moving steadily without their wings,
ignoring publicly the cries of their young,
too scared the screaming vulture will come.
Who? Who are you?
We see the clipped senators' spirits starting to die.

Chaos

How come you open up your mouth
and say what I have done?
Put down your pen and paper and yield, fools.
We will find a back door and climb up your ladder.
We will cut you up and lock you down.
Put down your pen and paper,
do not say my name or we will cover you up in my snow.
I have the keys; you gave them to me.
I came through the front door and I will lock you out.
I am here. I feel free. I am here for me.
You should be here for me, so put down your pen and paper,
leave your clicks behind or I will lock you out.
You do for me and I will do for you.
To the people behind me: Stay silent;
Do not backslide or you, too, will be cut down.
You may cry, you may laugh, but I will eat and swallow.
You can clean up later.
I am not here to hurt you; neither am I here to serve you,
I am here to tell you and to replace you.
I am here to create doubt and chaos.
I am here to take away your friends up to your very end.
I am your President.

POTUS and POTO

Why do they chase me, these younglings?
Why not turn a brown eye,
make a mark as you are told--
somewhere in the room next door.
I watched you walking, talking and scouting around,
crusading and awakening the many.
But my desires are not so—let them sleep—remove yourselves,
discard your truth and let them hear me.
I am POTUS, my words are heavy and my truth flexible.
Reap what's given to you.
Do not try to plant seeds in people's hearts--
that ground is mine.
Be silent; let them sleep.
I need more time. I will get more time.

The Problem with Truce

I negotiated a truce on Monday
Only to find them fighting on Tuesday.

Kneel

I saw the Supremes on their knees,
answering for their misdeeds,
the announcement was that they were supposed to lead.
But they sang the song of blind eyes and left the country to bleed.
Now the Bible Belters are at the altar,
with the Supremes on their knees.
Kneel!
and feel what I feel.

Union Station

I watched the trail of bread crumbs as I entered the DC station,
little cords of flashing lights attached to them.
My feet spasmodically kicked one and eyes looked up at me,
then went back to sleep.
My son and nephew were with me,
two years nine months, and five.
Cautiously, they avoided the crumbs, asking,
"Mommy aunty, where are their beds?"
My mind said, "Ask the president,"
but I answered them sincerely.
"Thank God for a place to live."
There weren't any insects or wind or witches,
but the multicolored bread crumbs kept moving in place.
An inch or two, then back; nobody wanted them--
not the insects, not the wind, not the wicked witch.
I reached the last crumb and eyes looked up at me and said nothing,
crumb too young to speak.
I exited the station.

The Proof

Show me what you said I've done.
Show me the proof of your carnage
other than written words.
Your great grandfather long ago said we did it.
My great grandmother said that we didn't.
Where is your proof?
"My grandmother burned it."

Wings

I tried to fly away today
but I could not find my wings.
Every time I heard a call, my arm began to swing.
I checked my mind then started to cry,
but no wings came falling by,
I got some glue and a couple of screws,
Then made more wings than two.
My neighbor came over and my sisters too,
then other women and Sue.
When evening came and we heard our names,
we grabbed our wings and flew.
We flew away! That's the truth,
that's why I am talking to you.

Angels on My Pages

There is an angel
who sits on the top of my poetry pages.
He smiles upon you as you read,
offering you clarity and joy.
I do not ask him why he is here,
for blessings given are blessings taken.
I wondered out aloud one day,
"You are so close to the edge. Will you not fall?"
But the angel smiled and said,
"I will not fall off your pages."
"A small dot of space from your pen is all that I need."
I wrote and wrote then I had to ask,
"How will people know that you are here?"
"By opening their own hearts and making us a small dot of space." He replied.

Terryann

“One line,” I said, “Just one line.”
She paused, then paused some more.
Then she started to sing
a song I did not know,
a song I did not believe I had ever heard.
As she sang, her voice penetrated the listeners’ minds and bodies.
It penetrated the metal which gave way.

There was a man of about 25 years,
I wanted him to hear her sing,
but as her voice lifted and her song elevated,
he crumbled and I do not know where he went.
He was almost tall, he was slender.
He wore clean khaki clothing,
he never told me his given name, but he was a pastor.

The song she sang broke through me.
I felt and saw the cloudiness of my faith lifted,
I grew wings: big, strong, unbreakable wings.
Fear and business were gone from my mind.
Doubt and the clogging of my spirit were gone.
I flapped my arms, my wings; I could fly
and I knew I would not fall, that I could not fail.
I flew above the people. Everyone seemed busy.

I perched on the side of a building; it was concrete.
I examined my claws, powerful and strong.
My wings appeared ash gray without and snow white within,
my wings were soft and warm and my sight was clear.
I turned my head and looked below,

There, I saw a lady smiling and waving at me.

Her dress was gray and she wore a white scarf.
I knew her--that was me.
One of my feathers fell and she picked it up.
The singing had stopped and I still did not know the name of that song,
but I could feel it beneath my bone. I can fly.
And the voice of that song was Terryann.

Lullaby

God be with you little child of mine,
Wherever you go whatever you do.
God be with you little child of mine,
Whatever you say in this life of yours.
God be with you little child of mine,
Wherever you go in this life of mine.

Safe

I have a place I would like to make,
put it on a plate and let's create
a state that's safe.
Think hard and concentrate.

God Bless America

God bless America for the birds and the bees
God bless America for my tainted cheese
God bless America for the die-hards
God bless America for the dirty bastards
God bless America for credit cards
God bless America for the immigrants and pines
God bless us all for He is divine.

Sweet City Cares

In Sweet City, there is a little boy.
He likes chocolate very much, as well as toys.
He built a bridge to his city and it's free for everyone.
That city he named Sweet City.
In the city, there is much to enjoy:
Cars and sharks, soldiers and bulldozers,
cherry pie and helicopters to fly,
the roads are chocolate,
the water is chocolate,
but most seriously, the pizza and people are made of chocolate.
Come to my city because Sweet City Cares.

GALLERY

Tree Song: Painting by Andrea Elizabeth De Graaf

Can Someone Find Me: Painting by Andrea Elizabeth De Graaf

If You Find Me: Painting by Andrea Elizabeth De Graaf

Decline : Painting by Tia Nesbeth

Scrappy Babies: Painting by Andrea Elizabeth De Graaf

Insurance Lost: Painting by Andrea Elizabeth De Graaf

Detained Sight: Photograph by Algria Simpson

Silas: Painting by Colette Morgan

Preformed Heart: Painting by Andrea Elizabeth De Graaf

The Watchman: Painting by Andrea Elizabeth De Graaf

Give Him Back: Photograph by Andrea Elizabeth De Graaf

Into Tomorrow: Painting by Andrea Elizabeth De Graaf

Into Tomorrow II: Illustration by Jude Morgan

The Catch: Photograph by Colette Morgan

Color You: Painting by Andrea Elizabeth De Graaf

To My Lady with the Freckles: Sketch by Andrea Elizabeth De Graaf

I Am Black: Painting by Andrea Elizabeth De Graaf

Senators on the Branch: Photograph by Andrea Elizabeth De Graaf

Chaos: Design by Andrea Elizabeth De Graaf

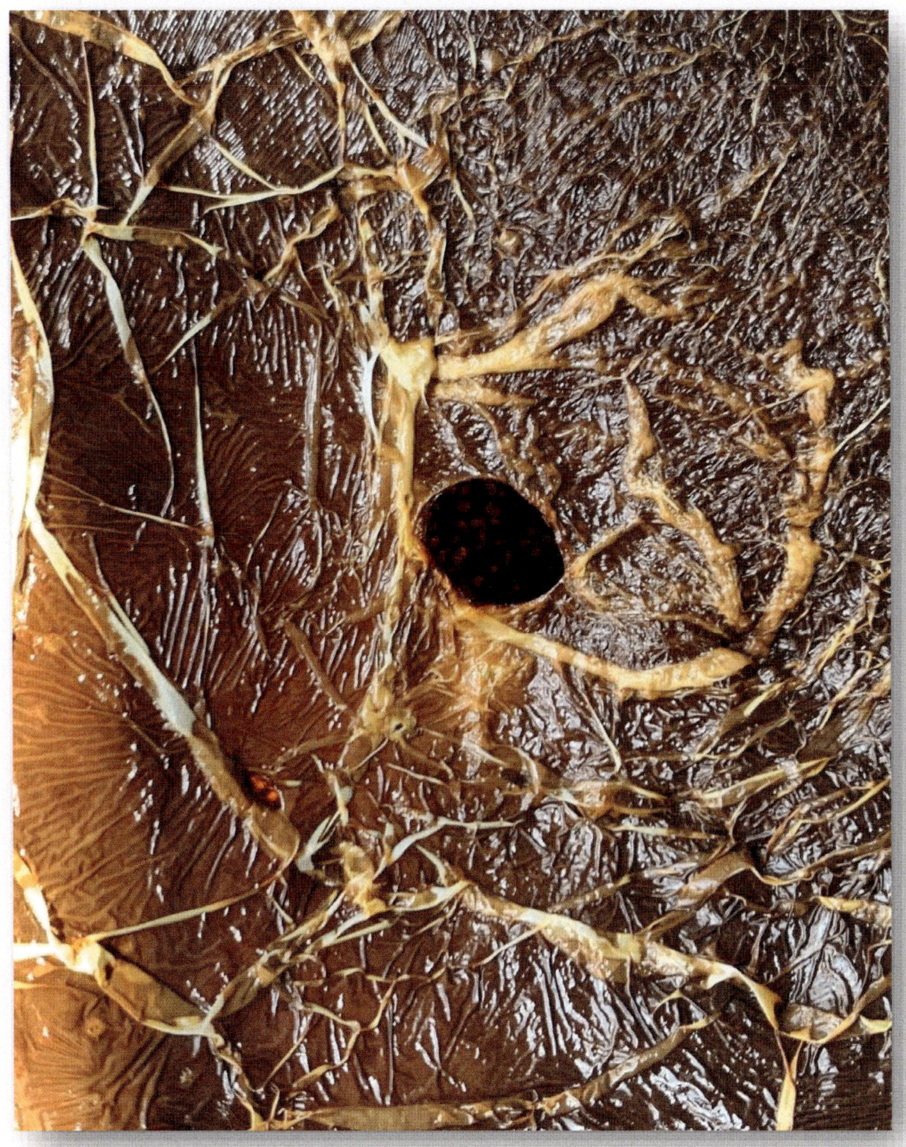

POTUS and POTO: Illustration by Andrea Elizabeth De Graaf

Union Station: Painting by Andrea Elizabeth De Graaf

Angels on My Pages: Painting by Andrea Elizabeth De Graaf

Terryann: Illustration by Colette Morgan

Lullaby: Photograph by Andrea Elizabeth De Graaf

God Bless America: Drawings by Vincent Rene De Graaf

Sweet City Cares: Illustration by Vincent Rene De Graaf

SPECIAL THANKS

Special thanks to Animator/Illustrator Steven A. Johnson (SAJ-man) for all of his tireless time spent on working through the layout and formation of this book, and, for so many other creative ideas as well.

ACKNOWLEDGEMENTS

To my husband Kai De Graaf; thank you for making me tea whenever I seemed stuck on a page *of Sweet City Care*, whenever I was just rubbing my head or whenever you saw me. Thank you for your constant support and for giving me the opportunity, the uninterrupted time to write and put this book together. I must also thank my son Vincent for each evening reminding me to write. To my sisters: Colette, Darien, Maureen, Algria and Royana, thank you for being the best source of strength for me to draw from. To my brothers, thank you for teaching me how to deal with different temperaments. To my nieces, Titania and Tia, and my nephews, Reco and Shaquille; you listened to my poems endlessly before bedtime you helped me to realize that small children are not just around to be taken care of, but to shine light in our darkest corners for us to see. To my niece Judine, I will definitely vote for you, and niece Terryann, your voice gave me the clarity of mind and spirit to fly, whenever I needed. Renee you are the best. To my cousin, Dawn Scott Wright; thank you for providing a safe place for me to develop my writing skills and for teaching me not to run from anyone. To my parents, Sylvia and Clarence Morgan, everything I was, am, and will be is because of you, through God's blessings. With God, all things are possible.

ABOUT THE AUTHOR

Andrea Elizabeth De Graaf is the author of *Sweet City Cares.* She obtained a Bachelor of Arts Degree from Hunter College of the City University of New York, and a Master of Science in Administration at Central Michigan University.

This is Andrea's second poetry book.
She currently resides in Grand Rapids, Michigan USA.

Andrea's previous book *Natural Time A Poetry Collection* is available on Amazon.

Made in the USA
Monee, IL
22 December 2021